The Quotation Bank

Frankenstein

Mary Shelley

Copyright © 2020 Esse Publishing Limited

First published in 2020 by:
The Quotation Bank
Esse Publishing Limited

10 9 8 7 6 5 4 3 2 1

A CIP catalogue record for this book is available from the British Library.
ISBN 978-1-9999816-4-8

All enquiries to: contact@thequotationbank.co.uk

Printed and bound by Target Print Limited, Broad Lane, Cottenham, Cambridge CB24 8SW.

www.thequotationbank.co.uk

Introduction

Quotations

Revision and Essay Planning

Welcome to The Quotation Bank, the comprehensive guide to all the key quotations you need to succeed in your exams.

Whilst you may have read the novel, watched a film adaptation, understood the plot and have a strong grasp of context, the vast majority of marks awarded in your GCSEs are for the ability to write a focused essay, full of quotations, and most importantly, quotations that you then analyse.

I think we all agree it is **analysis** that is the tricky part – and that is why we are here to help!

The Quotation Bank takes 25 of the most important quotations from the text, interprets them, analyses them, highlights literary techniques Shelley has used, puts them in context, and suggests which quotations you might use in which essays.

At the end of **The Quotation Bank** we have put together a sample answer, essay plans and great revision exercises to help you prepare for your exam. We have also included a detailed glossary to make sure you completely understand what certain literary terms actually mean!

English Literature 9-1: What are examiners looking for?

All GCSE Exam Boards mark your exams using the same Assessment Objectives (AOs) – around 80% of your mark across the English Literature GCSE will be awarded for AO1 and AO2.

AO1	Read, understand and respond to texts. Students should be able to: • Maintain a critical style and develop an *informed personal response* • Use textual references, *including quotations*, to support and illustrate *interpretations*.
AO2	Analyse the *Language, Form and Structure* used by a writer to *create meanings and effects*, using *relevant subject terminology* where appropriate.

Basically, **AO1** is the ability to answer the question set, showing a good knowledge of the text, and using quotations to back up ideas and interpretations.

AO2 is the ability to analyse these quotations, as well as the literary techniques the writer uses, and to show you understand the effect of these on the reader.

We will also highlight elements of **AO3** – the context in which the novel is set.

How The Quotation Bank can help you in your exams.

The Quotation Bank is designed to make sure that every point you make in an essay clearly fulfils the Assessment Objectives an examiner will be using when marking your work.

Every quotation comes with the following detailed material:

Interpretation: The interpretation of each quotation allows you to fulfil **AO1**, responding to the text and giving an informed personal response.

Techniques: Using subject-specific terminology correctly (in this case, the literary devices used by Shelley) is a key part of **AO2**.

Analysis: We have provided as much analysis (**AO2**) as possible. It is a great idea to analyse the quotation in detail – you need to do more than just say what it means, but also what effect the language, form and structure has on the reader.

Use in essays on… Your answer needs to be focused to fulfil **AO1**. This section helps you choose relevant quotations and link them together for a stronger essay.

How to use The Quotation Bank.

Many students spend time learning quotations by heart.

This is an excellent idea, but they often forget what they are meant to do with those quotations once they get into the exam!

By using **The Quotation Bank**, not only will you have a huge number of quotations to use in your essays, you will also have ideas on what to say about them, how to analyse them, how to link them together, and what questions to use them for.

For GCSE essay questions, these quotations can form the basis of your answer, making sure every point comes **directly from the text (AO1)** and allowing you to **analyse language, form and structure (AO2)**. We also highlight where you can easily and effectively include **context (AO3)**.

For GCSE questions that give you an extract to analyse, the quotations in **The Quotation Bank** are excellent not only for revising the skills of **analysis (AO2)**, but also for showing **wider understanding of the text (AO1)**.

Letter One:

"Its productions and features may be without example, as the phenomena of the heavenly bodies undoubtedly are in those undiscovered solitudes. What may not be expected in a country of eternal light?"

Interpretation: Walton depicts exploration as an activity that shines light upon the world, almost spiritual in nature, full of "productions", "features" and "phenomena".

Techniques: Tone; Metaphor; Allusion.

Analysis:

- The association of scientific discovery with "heavenly bodies" bestows a spiritual significance upon Walton's exploration – Walton does not see a potential conflict between scientific discovery and religious teachings.
- The optimistic tone of "undiscovered", "without example" and "be expected" is somewhat naïve – Walton does not consider that his discoveries would be anything other than positive and cannot conceive the horrors that are to come.
- "Eternal light" acts as a metaphor for scientific exploration. "Eternal" implies the endless advancement of human knowledge, "light" depicts the "undiscovered" being brought into view, whilst the allusion to the biblical "eternal light" further enhances the relationship between God and discovery.

Use in essays on… Ambition; Pursuit of Knowledge; Religion; Nature and the Sublime.

Letter Two:
"I desire the company of a man who could sympathise with me, whose eyes would reply to mine. You may deem me romantic, my dear sister, but I bitterly feel the want of a friend."

Interpretation: Foreshadowing the monster's demand for "a creature of another sex", Walton highlights the innate human need for companionship and communication.

Techniques: Adverb; Tone; Foreshadowing.

Analysis:

- The adverb "bitterly" conveys the pain of isolation; his desperate tone alongside the aggression of "want" foreshadows the monster's brutal response to his own isolation, implying this reaction was not evil, but rather it was entirely natural.
- A "friend" prevents loneliness ("company"), provides emotional support ("sympathise") and intimate human connection ("eyes would reply"), all concepts the monster desperately seeks later in the novel.
- "Romantic" implies companionship is full of warmth and humanity, traits Frankenstein does not see in the monster when he demands a mate for himself.

Use in essays on…Family; Exclusion and Isolation; Pursuit of Knowledge.

Letter Four:
"One man's life or death were but a small price to pay for the acquirement of the knowledge which I sought, for the dominion I should acquire and transmit over the elemental foes of our race."

Interpretation: Whether the "one man" Walton refers to is himself or a member of his expedition, he clearly shares Frankenstein's belief that knowledge transcends life itself.

Techniques: Alliteration; Personification; Allusion.

Analysis:
- The emotional impact of "life or death" is flippantly dismissed as "small", with the alliterative "price to pay" rapidly moving past the sacrifice of "one man".
- Walton views life as a battle between humanity and nature; "elemental" components are personified as "foes", implying innate conflict within the world.
- "Knowledge" alludes to Eve, who "sought" to eat from the tree of knowledge. Walton sees life as a war between "foes" but fails to see his "acquirement" of "knowledge", much like Eve's, brings sin to the world. He desires "dominion" and to "transmit over", both conveying repression and abuse of power.

Use in essays on…Life and Death; Power and Responsibility; Pursuit of Knowledge.

Chapter 1:
"I was their plaything and their idol, and something better – their child, the innocent and helpless creature bestowed on them by Heaven."

Interpretation: Frankenstein dwells on the love a parent has for their own child, and the repetition of "their" focuses on the duty a parent has towards a child they conceived.

Techniques: Irony; Repetition.

Analysis:
- The pleasurable associations of "plaything" evoke the joy that bringing life into the world creates, whilst "idol" implies a sense of worship and adoration.
- A "child" is elevated above this joy and adoration as it was "bestowed on them by Heaven" – when a child is naturally conceived, as opposed to Frankenstein's unnatural creation, it is a beautiful spiritual gift from God.
- "Innocent" and "helpless" imply Frankenstein understands the vulnerability of a new-born child; ironically, defining himself as a "creature" conveys his animalistic need for protection, yet he does not bestow the same protection upon his own creation later in the novel.

Use in essays on…Religion; Family; Exclusion and Isolation.

Chapter 2:

"The world was to me a secret which I desired to divine. Curiosity, earnest research to learn the hidden laws of nature, gladness akin to rapture, as they were unfolded to me, are among the earliest sensations I can remember."

Interpretation: Frankenstein's desire for education and discovery is seemingly pure, driven by an insatiable thirst for knowledge, yet it clearly has a powerful hold on him.

Techniques: Alliteration; Juxtaposition.

Analysis:

- "Curiosity" implies a healthy interest in "the world", with "earnest research" and "unfolded" reinforcing a rational, methodical approach to his studies.
- However, "secret" and "hidden" depict a desire to go beyond the bounds of acceptable social norms – whilst "gladness" implies moderation, the juxtaposition with "rapture" implies "sensations" will soon overwhelm him.
- Whilst "divine" means to understand, it also has associations with heavenly behaviour, yet the alliterative 'd' sound links the purity of "divine" with the lustful connotations of "desired", corrupting its meaning.

Use in essays on… Nature and the Sublime; Pursuit of Knowledge; Ambition.

Chapter 3:

> "Chance—or rather the evil influence, the Angel of Destruction, which asserted omnipotent sway over me from the moment I turned my reluctant steps from my father's door."

Interpretation: In the early stages of his tale, Frankenstein uses his power as narrator to lay the blame for the horrors to come on "chance", "influence" and "sway".

Techniques: Personification; Language.

Analysis:
- "My reluctant steps" implies a nervousness about his decision to leave, but the use of "I turned" and "my" both imply Frankenstein's active choice at moving on from the safety of "my father's door".
- However, Frankenstein refuses to take responsibility for his actions; he blames fate ("chance"), the devil ("evil influence") and religion ("Angel of Destruction").
- Religion is depicted as cruel and oppressive – the "Angel of Destruction" destroys rather than creates life, and the aggressive tone of "asserted omnipotent sway" depicts an oppressive, controlling deity.

Use in essays on…Religion; Power and Responsibility; Violence.

Chapter 4:
"After so much time spent in painful labour, to arrive at once at the summit of my desires was the most gratifying consummation of my toils."

Interpretation: Frankenstein explores what it means to create life. He uses the language of natural childbirth to depict his ability to bestow "animation upon lifeless matter".

Techniques: Allusion; Semantic Field; Tone.

Analysis:
- Whilst "painful labour" and "consummation" here refer to the hard work Frankenstein puts into his studies, they also come from the semantic field of childbirth. By alluding to natural birth, Shelley illuminates the unnatural elements of Frankenstein's work.
- Although "summit" conveys a grand purpose to his experiments, "painful" and "toils" create a tone of negativity and suffering around his work.
- Indeed, "desires" and "gratifying" suggest the motivation for this study is not for the benefit of society, but rather for his own selfish pleasures, regardless of the "painful" consequences. He is going against God's will for his own gain.

Use in essays on... Life and Death; Ambition; Pursuit of Knowledge.

Chapter 5:

"His jaws opened, and he muttered some inarticulate sounds, while a grin wrinkled his cheeks. He might have spoken, but I did not hear; one hand was stretched out, seemingly to detain me."

Interpretation: The reader's view of the monster comes from Frankenstein's biased narration. Whilst clearly terrifying, there is much humanity to be found in the monster.

Techniques: Imagery; Narrative Voice.

Analysis:

- "Jaws" depicts the monster as animalistic – "inarticulate sounds" convey a lack of intelligence and humanity. However, the fault lies with Frankenstein; the monster sought to communicate ("spoken") and Frankenstein "did not hear".

- "Seemingly" stresses the prejudice of Frankenstein; he interprets a "grin" as threatening, and a "stretched out" hand as trying "to detain me", reinforcing the predatorial associations of "jaws".

- However, a "hand...stretched out", "inarticulate sounds", and a "grin wrinkled his cheeks", could be interpreted as the playful actions of a vulnerable new-born seeking interaction and security from a parent.

Use in essays on... Violence; Life and Death; Family; Exclusion and Isolation.

Chapter 6:

> "Justine, thus received in our family, learned the duties of a servant, a condition which, in our fortunate country, does not include the idea of ignorance and a sacrifice of the dignity of a human being."

Interpretation: There is an irony and hypocrisy to Frankenstein's words; he appreciates that, in a "fortunate country", "dignity" is a right that should be bestowed on all people, yet he denies dignity to the monster.

Techniques: Irony; Alliteration; Abstract Nouns.

Analysis:

- "Received" implies "our family" were willing to accept someone different from themselves, an act of welcome that was not bestowed upon the monster.

- The alliteration of "idea of ignorance" stresses that "ignorance" is an "idea", not a natural state – the monster "learned the duties" of humankind later in the novel, but his "condition" meant he was rejected by all he met.

- The monster only ever wants friendship, love and "dignity", abstract concepts that can be given easily and freely – not only does he not receive them from Frankenstein, but the De Lacey family, who happily "received in our family" the foreign Safie, also reject him.

Use in essays on… Family; Exclusion and Isolation.

Chapter 7:

"Who would believe, unless his senses convinced him, in the existence of the living monument of presumption and rash ignorance which I had let loose upon the world?"

Interpretation: Ambition can be a positive trait that expands the limits of human knowledge; however, if not tempered with rational sense, the consequences can be tragic.

Techniques: Metaphor; Alliteration; Allusion.

Analysis:

- The metaphor of a "living monument" stresses not only the long-term consequences of Frankenstein's actions ("monument"), but also conveys the present nature of the threat ("living").

- "Monument" should represent the pinnacle of achievement, yet this monument represents the unbelievable ("who would believe") and irrational ("senses convinced him") decisions Frankenstein took.

- The alliteration of "let loose" mimics the swiftness with which the situation escalated, and "loose" implies a complete lack of control – the threat to "the world" is made all the more damning through the petty and foolish associations of "presumption" and "rash ignorance" which caused them.

Use in essays on…Power and Responsibility; Ambition.

Chapter 8:
"I believe that I have no enemy on earth, and none surely would have been so wicked as to destroy me wantonly."

Interpretation: Justine's innocence, both in a religious sense and of the crime she is accused of, heightens the reader's sympathy towards her.

Techniques: Sentence Structure; Alliteration; Semantic Field.

Analysis:
- The phrase "no enemy on earth" conveys the magnitude of Frankenstein's sin. His unnatural creation of life is beyond "earth" in its evil, implying it is a sin that originates from hell ("wicked").
- The sentence structure stresses "surely", which accentuates the difference between Frankenstein and the innocent Justine – whilst he sought to push the boundaries of knowledge, she cannot begin to comprehend such evil.
- Language from a semantic field of suffering and conflict ("enemy", "wicked", "destroy" and "wantonly") are all the more painful for the reader as they are spoken by a character as pure as Justine.

Use in essays on…Violence; Life and Death; Religion.

Chapter 9:
"Immense glaciers approached the road; I heard the rumbling thunder of the falling avalanche and marked the smoke of its passage. Mont Blanc, the supreme and magnificent Mont Blanc, raised itself from the surrounding *aiguilles*, and its tremendous *dôme* overlooked the valley."

Interpretation: Frankenstein dedicated his life to giving humans control over the natural world, yet the sublime power of Mont Blanc depicts nature's unconquerable greatness.

Techniques: Setting; Personification; Allusion.

Analysis:
- "Supreme" bestows a spiritual power upon Mont Blanc, with "overlooked" depicting it as an omnipresent God, yet "rumbling thunder" alludes to the more threatening, wrathful side of God, one who should not be challenged.
- Frankenstein originally saw nature as "lifeless matter", yet the personification of nature as it "raised itself" confirms the error of his original hypothesis.
- Rather than something man can control, the sublime nature of the setting with "immense glaciers", "falling avalanche" and the "magnificent Mont Blanc" and "its tremendous *dôme*" highlights the insurmountable scale of the natural world.

Use in essays on…Nature and the Sublime; Religion.

Chapter 10:

"On you it rests, whether I quit for ever the neighbourhood of man and lead a harmless life, or become the scourge of your fellow creatures and the author of your own speedy ruin."

Interpretation: Walton and Frankenstein desire immense knowledge and power, but the monster highlights the responsibility and consequences that accompany such choices.

Techniques: Imagery; Language.

Analysis:

- "On you it rests" stresses a key contemporary debate around scientific experimentation – although Frankenstein proved he could animate "lifeless matter", he failed to fully consider the ethical, moral and spiritual consequences.
- The image of a "neighbourhood of man" evokes the idea of companionship and the communal existence that makes us human – the fact the monster recognises this emphasises his humanity.
- "Scourge" and "ruin" convey the monster's evil, yet "harmless life" implies he is capable of virtue, "author" indicates his intellectual mind, and "creatures" suggests that man and monster are all essentially animalistic in nature.

Use in essays on… Power and Responsibility; Exclusion and Isolation; Violence.

Chapter 11:

> "I was a poor, helpless, miserable wretch; I knew, and could distinguish, nothing; but feeling pain invade me on all sides, I sat down and wept."

Interpretation: The eloquence and humanity of the monster's narration evokes great sympathy from the reader – his weeping and "feeling" depict him as entirely human.

Techniques: Tri-colon; Imagery.

Analysis:

- The tri-colon "poor, helpless, miserable" accentuates the monster's suffering – rather than "wretch" implying a despicable creature, "wretch" conveys him as someone vulnerable ("helpless") and suffering terribly ("miserable").
- Although full of the ignorance ("nothing") of infancy, the monster displays great sensitivity and awareness ("knew" and "distinguish") of his situation – the image of "sat down and wept" vividly portrays his emotional vulnerability.
- "Feeling pain" conveys his humanity, with militaristic associations of "invade" depicting the violence inherent in the world – "on all sides" highlights the all-encompassing nature of this violence.

Use in essays on…Exclusion and Isolation; Life and Death.

Chapter 12:
"A considerable period elapsed before I discovered one of the causes of the uneasiness of this amiable family: it was poverty, and they suffered that evil in a very distressing degree."

Interpretation: The monster is acutely aware of the causes and injustices of human suffering, increasing the reader's sympathy towards him when he is so cruelly rejected.

Techniques: Alliteration; Language.

Analysis:
- The monster's intellect is evident – "considerable period" implies dedicated study, with "discovered" asserting his ability to analyse human behaviours.
- He also displays great empathy and humanity – "amiable" recognises the love within the De Lacey family, and he feels anger towards the "evil" they suffer due to "poverty" and "uneasiness".
- The alliterative "distressing degree" emphasises the fact that society can cause as much suffering as the monster is capable of, but also implies the monster is capable of great empathy, a distinctly human attribute.

Use in essays on…Family; Exclusion and Isolation; Pursuit of Knowledge.

Chapter 13:
"Was man, indeed, at once so powerful, so virtuous and magnificent, yet so vicious and base?"

Interpretation: Having previously been "inarticulate", the monster now astutely questions the dual nature of mankind, conveying his sensitive, perceptive mind.

Techniques: Repetition; Juxtaposition; Questioning.

Analysis:

- Much of the turmoil in the novel stems from an inability to remain moderate; repetition of the intensifier "so" conveys mankind's inability to deal with extremes of emotion or to find balance between conflicting ideals.
- Conflict between science and religion, between man and nature, desire and self-control, permeates the novel. Repetition of the 'v' sound stresses the conflict between man's ability to be "virtuous" and at the same time "vicious", destructive and full of hate.
- "Man" is innately "powerful", but there is a fine line when using such power – whilst Frankenstein's original desire was to create something "magnificent", without responsibility that power quickly created something "base".

Use in essays on…Religion; Power and Responsibility; Violence.

Chapter 15:

"He had come forth from the hands of God a perfect creature, happy and prosperous, guarded by the especial care of his Creator; he was allowed to converse with and acquire knowledge from beings of a superior nature, but I was wretched, helpless, and alone."

Interpretation: By directly referencing Adam and the creation story, the monster makes explicit the blasphemous nature of Frankenstein's work in trying to become a "Creator".

Techniques: Tri-colon; Imagery; Adjectives.

Analysis:

- The image of Adam as a "creature" implies that, at a fundamental level, man and monster are essentially animals; it is how we are nurtured that dictates our behaviour.
- "Guarded" implies a protective "creator"; "allowed to converse" and "acquire knowledge" depict a creator that helps their creation grow and flourish in safety.
- "Happy" (conveying contentment) and "prosperous" (implying fulfilled potential) stress the responsibility a parent has in nurturing a child. By rejecting the monster, Frankenstein not only neglects his responsibility to science, but also causes isolation ("alone"), vulnerability ("helpless") and pain ("wretched").

Use in essays on…Religion; Power and Responsibility; Exclusion and Isolation; Family.

Chapter 16:

"I gazed on my victim, and my heart swelled with exultation and hellish triumph; clapping my hands, I exclaimed, 'I too can create desolation; my enemy is not invulnerable; this death will carry despair to him, and a thousand other miseries shall torment and destroy him.'"

Interpretation: Whilst often sympathetic, here the monster displays diabolic traits, taking pleasure in the suffering and despair he creates in the taking of an innocent life.

Techniques: Imagery; Oxymoron; Semantic Field.

Analysis:

- Joyous images of "heart swelled with exultation" and "clapping my hands" as he "gazed" accentuate the demonic nature of the monster. "Hellish" alludes to his devilish "triumph" over the vulnerable, innocent victim William.

- The oxymoronic "create desolation" encapsulates the unseen consequences of men who try to play God; by trying to generate life, Frankenstein causes death.

- The reference to "enemy" and a semantic field of suffering ("despair", "miseries", "torment" and "destroy") recalls the battle between God and Satan in the original creation story, heightening the monster's devilish qualities.

Use in essays on…Violence; Power and Responsibility; Life and Death; Family.

Chapter 17:

> " "I swear," he cried, "by the sun, and by the blue sky of heaven, and by the fire of love that burns my heart, that if you grant my prayer, while they exist you shall never behold me again." "

Interpretation: The reader shares Frankenstein's fear of creating a new monster, but the monster conveys a desperate vulnerability for a "fire of love" that evokes great sympathy.

Techniques: Irony; Language.

Analysis:

- There is a purity to the monster's spiritual nature - he swears upon "the sun", a symbol of life, and "blue sky of heaven", which alludes to natural ("blue sky") and religious ("heaven") perfection.
- There is an intensity to the monster's cry, but "fire" and "burns" are not destructive; instead they bring forth "love" from "his heart", further accentuating his humanity.
- Ironically, in asking Frankenstein to "grant my prayer", the monster deifies his creator and elevates him to the status of a god, yet rather than move humanity forward, he creates isolation and loneliness ("never behold me again").

Use in essays on…Religion; Nature and the Sublime; Power and Responsibility.

Chapter 19:
   "When these thoughts possessed me, I would not quit Henry for a moment, but followed him as his shadow, to protect him from the fancied rage of his destroyer."

Interpretation: Frankenstein brutally rejects the monster and abandons him to his fate, in juxtaposition with the intense protection, adoration and love he shows Henry here.

Techniques: Language; Imagery.

Analysis:
- One of Frankenstein's failings is his refusal to care for the monster he created – however, it is clear he is capable of intensely paternal instincts, with "would not quit", "followed" and "protect him" all conveying a desire to keep Henry safe.
- In one way, becoming Henry's "shadow" depicts the intimacy of the relationship between the two, yet "shadow" could also imply that Frankenstein has been reduced to a "shadow" of his former vibrant, dynamic self.
- Frankenstein's life is devoid of spiritual or natural salvation. He is "possessed", suggesting a diabolic quality; love and tenderness is replaced by "fancied rage"; and images of creation are under attack from a "destroyer".

Use in essays on…Violence; Family; Life and Death; Power and Responsibility.

Chapter 20:
"I can make you so wretched that the light of day will be hateful to you. You are my creator, but I am your master; obey!"

Interpretation: The monster's violence and murders accentuate his "hateful" character, but the reader must question whether this is as a result of nature or nurture.

Techniques: Imperative; Imagery.

Analysis:

- The monster's threat to "make you so wretched" is evil and enhances his inhuman characteristics, yet ironically it is no different to the "wretched" manner in which he is treated by all humankind.
- There is a diabolic quality to the monster – "light of day" is an image of spiritual purity, yet he intends to corrupt it into something "hateful".
- Walton earlier sought "dominion" through knowledge, and Frankenstein naively believed his creation would "bless me as its creator", yet neither become a "master" – the imperative "obey!" confirms true "dominion" stems from the monster's ability to destroy life, not create it.

Use in essays on… Violence; Power and Responsibility; Life and Death.

27

Chapter 21:
"Have my murderous machinations deprived you also, my dearest Henry, of life? Two I have already destroyed; other victims await their destiny; but you, Clerval, my friend, my benefactor—"

Interpretation: Both Walton and Frankenstein were blind to the consequences of their actions – Frankenstein finally admits his behaviour has led to murder and destruction.

Techniques: Alliteration; Questioning.

Analysis:

- The violent 'm' sound creates a tone of anger, with "machinations" diminishing the scientific validity of his original research, and "my murderous" implying Frankenstein has now taken responsibility for the consequences of his actions, accentuated by "I have".
- Both Walton and Frankenstein set out to "discover", yet rather than create knowledge they end up "deprived" and "destroyed".
- Walton previously asked "what can stop the determined heart and resolved will of man?", yet here Frankenstein has come to understand man is at the mercy of a higher being as "other victims await their destiny".

Use in essays on…Life and Death; Power and Responsibility; Family; Violence.

Chapter 22:

"Look also at the innumerable fish that are swimming in the clear waters, where we can distinguish every pebble that lies at the bottom. What a divine day! How happy and serene all nature appears!"

Interpretation: Elizabeth articulates the beauty present in the world; God's reasons for creating the world were pure, therefore unity and peace are evident in all Elizabeth sees.

Techniques: Alliteration; Semantic Field; Personification.

Analysis:

- Rather than the secrecy and darkness of Frankenstein's creation, the semantic field of sight ("look", "clear", "distinguish" and "appears") suggests legitimate creation never needs to be hidden from view.

- "Innumerable fish", "clear waters" and "every pebble" convey the abundance and scale of nature's brilliance; the alliterative "divine day" implies creation is God's domain, rather than the unnatural scientific explorations of mankind.

- Frankenstein may have produced life, but it brought nothing but suffering and pain – the personified "nature" is "happy and serene", implying creation of life is not simply a scientific concept, but involves emotion and tenderness.

Use in essays on…Nature and the Sublime; Religion; Pursuit of Knowledge.

Chapter 24:

> "Oh! Be men, or be more than men. Be steady to your purposes and firm as a rock."

Interpretation: Despite the horrors that befell Frankenstein, his need to "pioneer a new way, explore unknown powers" burns as strongly as it did upon his arrival at Ingolstadt.

Techniques: Alliteration; Tone; Simile; Repetition.

Analysis:

- Despite all that has happened to Frankenstein over the course of the novel, the passionate exclamation "Oh!" emphasises the resilience of his spirit.
- Whilst "be men" has a determined tone, the alliteration of "more than men" stresses Frankenstein's desire to exceed ("more than") the normal limits of human experience is still present, further reinforced by the repetition of a determination to "be".
- The simile "firm as a rock" and the use of "steady" both imply the importance of unbreakable dedication to one's "purposes"; however, the inflexible nature of "rock" suggests Frankenstein has still not learnt the importance of changing course when, like Walton's expedition, continuing on would be foolish.

Use in essays on…Ambition; Pursuit of Knowledge.

Chapter 24:
"**Evil thenceforth became my good. Urged thus far, I had no choice but to adapt my nature to an element which I had willingly chosen. The completion of my demoniacal design became an insatiable passion.**"

Interpretation: The novel ends as it begins; a creature driven towards a "design" by an "insatiable passion" they do not seem to be able to resist, no matter the consequences.

Techniques: Juxtaposition; Alliteration.

Analysis:
- Juxtaposition between "evil" and "good" depicts a binary choice between the "good" of God's word or "evil" sin. In testing the boundaries of knowledge, it could be argued both Frankenstein and Walton are moving away from God.
- "No choice" suggests the monster's behaviour is innate, yet "urged", "adapt" and "chosen" imply his decisions were nurtured by factors around him.
- "Demoniacal design" stresses "evil" in the monster's plan, and "insatiable passion" conveys irrational thought, yet Walton and Frankenstein are also guilty of "insatiable passion" for the "completion" of a "demoniacal design". Do we judge them as we do the monster, or are we somewhat hypocritical?

Use in essays on…Religion; Violence; Life and Death.

Major Themes

Ambition	Pursuit of Knowledge	Religion
Exclusion and Isolation	Power and Responsibility	Nature and the Sublime
Family	Life and Death	Violence

Major Characters

Victor Frankenstein	The Monster	Robert Walton
Henry Clerval	Elizabeth Lavenza	Justine Moritz
Alphonse Frankenstein and Caroline Beaufort	William Frankenstein	The De Lacey Family

How to revise effectively.

One mistake people often make is to try to revise EVERYTHING!

This is clearly not possible.

Instead, once you know and understand the plot, a great idea is to pick three or four major themes, and three or four major characters, and revise these in great detail.

If, for example, you revised Ambition and Religion, you will also have covered a huge amount of material to use in questions about Robert Walton or Power.

Or, if you revised Family and Frankenstein, you would certainly have plenty of material if a question on Exclusion and Isolation or The Monster came up.

Use the following framework as a basis for setting *any* of your own revision questions – simply swap the theme or character to create a new essay title!

How does Shelley portray the theme of _____in *Frankenstein*?

How does the character of _____ develop as the novel progresses?

A sample essay paragraph (top level), using ideas directly from The Quotation Bank (page 14).

How is the monster portrayed in Frankenstein?

Many of the reader's opinions of the monster come from Frankenstein's biased narration. Whilst clearly terrifying, there is much humanity to be found in the monster, seen immediately in his initial creation. Instinctively <u>"his jaws opened"</u>; <u>"jaws"</u> depicts the monster as animalistic, whilst his <u>"inarticulate sounds"</u> convey a lack of intelligence and humanity. However, the fault for the negative portrayal of the monster lies with Frankenstein; the monster sought to communicate, depicted clearly in the fact he had <u>"spoken"</u> and Frankenstein <u>"did not hear"</u>. In terms of the monster's actions, <u>"one hand was stretched out, seemingly to detain me"</u> - <u>"seemingly"</u> stresses the prejudice of Frankenstein and he interprets <u>"grin"</u> as threatening, with the <u>"stretched out"</u> hand trying <u>"to detain me"</u> reinforcing the predatorial associations of <u>"jaws"</u>. However, <u>"one hand was stretched out"</u>, <u>"muttered some inarticulate sounds"</u>, and a <u>"grin wrinkled his cheeks"</u>, could be the playful actions of a vulnerable new-born seeking interaction and security from a parent. In many ways, the monster is displaying the characteristics of a new-born infant whilst Frankenstein appears to be a neglectful father.

Potential Essay Questions

How is nature depicted in the novel?

Topic Sentence 1: Nature is depicted as something humanity desires to conquer.

Use: Pages 11 and 13.

Topic Sentence 2: Despite this desire to control, the natural world frequently inspires a sublime effect, overwhelming human thought.

Use: Pages 18 and 29.

Topic Sentence 3: There is a clear and intimate connection between nature and religion.

Use: Pages 7 and 25.

Topic Sentence 4: The external world cannot alter mankind's internal nature, no matter how destructive that nature may be.

Use: Pages 30 and 31.

How is the idea of family explored throughout the novel?

Topic Sentence 1: The traditional family unit is depicted as welcoming, loving and supportive.

Use: Pages 10 and 15.

Topic Sentence 2: One of the major roles of the family unit is to provide comfort in challenging times.

Use: Pages 21 and 29.

Topic Sentence 3: Despite the strength of family ties, family is often sacrificed in the pursuit of individual ambitions.

Use: Pages 8 and 12.

Topic Sentence 4: The loss of family, or suffering that is brought upon them, is truly heart-breaking.

Use: Pages 17 and 24.

How does the monster develop throughout *Frankenstein*?

Topic Sentence 1: It is evident to the reader that the monster has an animalistic and unnatural character.

Use: Pages 14 and 27.

Topic Sentence 2: However, throughout the novel the reader is presented with the monster's great capacity for humanity, empathy and philosophical thought.

Use: Pages 20 and 22.

Topic Sentence 3: It is also clear that the monster is highly intelligent, sophisticated and eloquent.

Use: Pages 23 and 25.

Topic Sentence 4: Ultimately, the monster is overcome by evil desire – arguably this is his natural state, yet it may also be a consequence of how he was nurtured.

Use: Pages 19 and 31.

How is the concept of responsibility conveyed in the novel?

Topic Sentence 1: The responsibility a person has, both to themselves and to others, is often obscured from view by the power of ambition.

Use: Pages 7 and 9.

Topic Sentence 2: The inability to see one's responsibilities can also arise from a sense of disgust at what one needs to take responsibility for.

Use: Pages 14 and 16.

Topic Sentence 3: There are situations that can arise where who is responsible for an outcome is ambiguous.

Use: Pages 27 and 31.

Topic Sentence 4: However, there are times when one's responsibilities are unequivocal.

Use: Pages 26 and 28.

Suggested Revision Activities

Major character and themes – Take any of the major characters and themes (see page 32 for a list) and group together quotations in sets of 2 or 3 to answer the following question: "How does the theme/character develop as the novel goes on?"

You should try to get 4 sets of quotations, giving you 8-12 overall.

A great cover and repeat exercise – Cover the whole page, apart from the quotation at the top. Can you now fill in the four sections in your exercise book without looking – Interpretations, Techniques, Analysis, Use in essays on…?

This also works really well as a revision activity with a friend – cover the whole card, apart from the quotation at the top. If you read out the quotation, can they tell you the four sections without looking – Interpretations, Techniques, Analysis, Use in essays on…?

"The Development Game" – **Pick any quotation at random from The Quotation Bank and use it to create an essay question, and then create a focused topic sentence to start the essay. Next, find another appropriate quotation to develop your idea even further.**

"The Contrast Game" – **Follow the same rules as The Development Game, but instead of finding a quotation to support your idea, find a quotation that can be used to start a counter-argument.**

Your very own Quotation Bank! **Using the same headings and format as The Quotation Bank, find 10 more quotations from throughout the text (select them from many different sections of the text to help develop whole text knowledge) and create your own revision cards.**

Essay writing – **They aren't always fun, but writing essays is great revision. Choose a practice question and then try taking three quotations and writing out a perfect paragraph, making sure you add connectives, technical vocabulary and sophisticated language.**

Glossary

Alliteration – Repetition of the same consonant or sound at the beginning of a number of words in a sentence to create emphasis: "let loose" mimics the swiftness with which the situation escalated.

Allusion – Referring to something in a sentence without mentioning it explicitly: the biblical "eternal light" further enhances the relationship between God and discovery.

Imagery – Figurative language that appeals to the senses of the reader: "heart swelled with exultation" accentuates the demonic nature of the monster.

Irony – A statement that suggests one thing but often has a contrary meaning: Frankenstein defining himself as "creature" conveys his animalistic need for protection, yet he does not bestow the same protection upon his own creation later in the novel.

Juxtaposition – Two ideas, images or words placed next to each other to create a contrasting effect: "evil" and "good" depict a binary choice between the "good" of God's word and "evil" sin.

Language – The vocabulary chosen to create effect.

Metaphor – A word or phrase used to describe something else so that the first idea takes on the associations of the second: a "living monument" stresses not only the long-term nature of the consequences of Frankenstein's actions ("monument"), but "living" also conveys the present nature of the threat.

Narrative Voice – The perspective (or 'voice') from which the story is told: the reader's view of the monster comes from Frankenstein's biased narration.

Oxymoron – A figure of speech where apparently contradictory terms appear together: "create desolation" encapsulates the unseen consequences of men who try to play God.

Personification – A non-human object or concept takes on human qualities to make its presence more vivid to the reader: "elemental" components are personified as "foes", implying innate conflict within the world.

Repetition – When a word, phrase or idea is repeated to reinforce it: the repetition of "their" focuses on the duty a parent has towards something they conceived.

Semantic Field – A group of words used together from the same topic area: the semantic field of sight ("look", "clear", "distinguish" and "appears") suggests legitimate creation never needs to be hidden from view.

Sentence Structure – The way the writer has ordered the words in a sentence to create a certain effect: a sentence structure stressing "surely" accentuates the difference between Frankenstein and the innocence of Justine.

Setting – The time, place and physical environment of where something takes place: "immense glaciers", "falling avalanche" and the "magnificent Mont Blanc" and "its tremendous *dôme*" highlights the insurmountable scale of the natural world.

Simile – A comparison of one thing with something of a different kind, used to make a description more vivid: "firm as a rock" implies the importance of unbreakable dedication to one's "purposes".

Tri-colon – A list of three words or phrases for effect: "poor, helpless, miserable" accentuates the monster's suffering.